SATCHEL
PAIGE

Julie Schmidt

For Jonas

Published in 2002 by The Rosen Publishing Group, Inc.
29 East 21st Street, New York, NY 10010

Library of Congress Cataloging-in-Publication Data

Schmidt, Julie.
Satchel Paige / by Julie Schmidt.— 1st ed.
p. cm. — (Baseball Hall of Famers of the Negro Leagues)
Includes bibliographical references and index.
ISBN 0-8239-3478-0 (lib. bdg.)
1. Paige, Leroy, 1906– —Juvenile literature. 2. Baseball players—
United States—Biography—Juvenile literature. 3. African American
baseball players—Biography—Juvenile literature. [1. Paige, Leroy,
1906– 2. Baseball players. 3. African Americans—Biography.]
I. Title. II. Series.
GV865.P3 S39 2002
796.357'092—dc21

2001003887

Manufactured in the United States of America

Contents

Though the integration of baseball came too late for most players his age, Satchel Paige made it to the major leagues in 1948 because he was still an effective pitcher at forty-two years old.

Introduction

I t was July 7, 1948. The day Satchel Paige had been waiting for his entire life had finally come. At long last, after two decades of professional pitching, the middle-aged black pitcher was being given a chance to try out for a major league team.

The team was the Cleveland Indians. Its owner, Bill Veeck, had long been a fan of Paige, and he wanted him for his team. However, the Indians' manager, Lou Boudreau, had his doubts about Paige's abilities. Paige had been a great pitcher in his day, but he was getting old. He also had a reputation for being wild and unreliable. Paige had to prove himself to this man if he wanted a spot on the team.

When Paige got out onto the field, Veeck and Boudreau were waiting. Boudreau asked Paige if he could still pitch. Paige admitted that he couldn't throw as fast as he used to, but he could still throw as fast as any other pitcher, and he had better control than anyone else. Veeck told him to prove it by pitching to Boudreau for ten minutes and trying to strike him out.

Boudreau asked Paige if he wanted to warm up first by running a lap or two. To please Boudreau, Paige ran a few steps, and then stopped—he had never liked running. The park was too big to run around, he explained, and he pitched with his arm, not with his feet.

Paige started to pitch, and every ball sailed right over the base into Boudreau's mitt. Then Paige decided he needed an extra challenge. In his typical cocky fashion, he stopped pitching, walked over to the plate, and laid a small handkerchief upon it. He then proceeded to put nine out of ten pitches over the handkerchief. According to some versions

Bill Veeck *(right)*, owner of the Cleveland Indians and a longtime supporter of Satchel Paige, convinced team manager Lou Boudreau *(left)* to hire Paige despite Boudreau's initial hesitation.

of this story, Paige threw four out of five fastballs directly over a cigarette placed on the ground. Paige was also said to have once thrown twenty consecutive pitches directly over a tiny gum wrapper. Some people say he learned his accuracy by using a bottle cap placed on the ground as a target. After Paige's amazing feat, Boudreau picked up a bat to see if he could hit Paige's pitches. The pitches were all different speeds and styles, but nineteen out of twenty of them were strikes.

After this spectacular display of talent, Boudreau had to admit that he had been wrong about Paige. He urged Veeck not to let him get away. That very day, Paige signed a contract to play with the Indians. The contract would make him the oldest rookie in major league history.

Paige was overjoyed. In his autobiography, he described making it to the majors as the greatest achievement of his life. This triumph, however, was only one of many in Paige's very distinguished career. His long, difficult, and exciting journey to the National Baseball Hall of Fame—a journey packed with dramatic highs and lows—had started four decades earlier, in Mobile, Alabama.

Out of Adversity

Nobody knows exactly when Leroy "Satchel" Paige was born. A birth certificate for a boy named Leroy Page, born on July 7, 1906, is filed in Mobile, Alabama, but Paige and his mother said they weren't sure that the birth certificate was his (a childhood friend, Ted "Double Duty" Radcliffe, claimed that Paige was born in 1900). The fact that no one knew exactly how old Satchel Paige was would make him mysterious and intriguing to his fans. It lent him an air of agelessness, as if he were immortal. And this impression was reinforced by his longevity as a powerful and skilled pitcher. Paige claimed to find the whole question of his age irrelevant to his abilities.

As he once remarked, "Age is a question of mind over matter. If you don't mind, it doesn't matter."

Although the date of his birth is uncertain, it is known that Leroy Paige's father, John, was a gardener, and his mother, Lula, was a laundress. John frequently left home and he did not contribute much to the family in the way of money. He died when Leroy was eighteen. It was Lula who was the main

This is a photo of a "shotgun" house, much like the one in which Satchel Paige spent his childhood in Mobile, Alabama.

The "Walking Satchel Tree"

Like other families in their neighborhood, the Paiges did not have much money, and Leroy had to work to help his mother buy food for the family. One of his jobs was to carry suitcases ("satchels") for passengers at the Mobile railway station. Leroy was paid ten cents a bag, and he wanted to make as much money as he could, so he rigged together a contraption consisting of a pole and some rope which allowed him to carry three or four bags at a time. He carried so many bags at once that the other porters said he looked like a "walking satchel tree." People say that is how Leroy got the nickname Satchel.

breadwinner. And it was Lula who was mostly responsible for raising the couple's twelve children. Lula was a strong-willed, church-going woman, and she tried hard to keep her children in line.

The Paiges lived in a four-room "shotgun" house (a long, narrow house in which all the rooms are lined up off to one side of a hallway) in a poor black neighborhood on the south side of Mobile. Life was hard for many black people in Mobile at this time. The city was segregated, and black residents had to deal with racist Jim Crow laws (which enforced segregation and other forms of racial discrimination) and limited opportunities to find good jobs.

Leroy was a student at the Council School, a school for black children, but he frequently skipped his classes. However, he did play baseball for his school team. Leroy had a powerful arm. He could throw rocks so hard that he once killed a chicken from thirty feet away. This strength and accuracy would prove to be very useful in his pitching career.

Unfortunately, while his baseball playing was improving, Leroy got into a lot of trouble off the field. Despite Lula's efforts to discipline him, he took part in many rock-throwing fights with neighborhood gangs. Usually, Leroy's black gang fought against a white gang from another neighborhood. Leroy became known as one of the most dangerous members of his gang because he could hit anyone at whom he aimed a rock.

When Leroy was twelve years old, he was caught stealing toy rings from a store. The storeowner took him to the police station, and Leroy was arrested. The court decided to send him to reform school. Leroy was sentenced to spend the rest of his childhood at the Industrial School for Negro Children at Mount Meigs, Alabama. At this time in the United States, "Negro" was the generally accepted term for African Americans. It comes from the Spanish word for "black." Both blacks and whites used it, and it did not yet carry racist connotations.

Turning Adversity into Opportunity

Leroy was frightened. It was the first time he had ever left home. He would not be allowed to visit his family in Mobile until his eighteenth birthday, which was still five years away. Also, he thought he might be treated badly at Mount Meigs by faculty and students alike. Strict discipline was enforced at the school, and students had to work in the fields for their keep.

Following his arrest, a young Satchel Paige was sentenced to the
Industrial School for Negro Children in Mount Meigs, Alabama,
a segregated reform school similar to the one pictured here.

Yet in later years, Leroy said that he considered himself lucky to have been sent to the school. Unlike at home, he was fed regular meals, and he got a lot of attention from the staff. In addition to his schoolwork, Leroy sang in the school choir, played the drums in the school band, and did woodworking. Most important, he played baseball.

The baseball coach at the Industrial School, Edward Byrd, soon discovered that he had a natural pitcher on his team. Leroy could not throw a curveball, but his fastball was hard and accurate. Byrd helped Leroy make his fastball even better.

Of his years in reform school, Leroy would later say, "It got me away from the bums. It gave me a chance to polish up my baseball game. It gave me some schooling I'd of never taken if I wasn't made to go to class."

Black and White Baseball

As he would do repeatedly throughout his life, at boarding school, Satchel Paige turned adversity to his advantage. In addition to receiving an education and much-needed adult attention at the Industrial School for Negro Children, it was there that he discovered the gift that would see him through the many long years ahead and establish him as a legend—his extraordinary skill as a pitcher.

First Job in Baseball

At the end of 1923, Paige was released from the Industrial School, and went back to Mobile. Paige's mother soon informed him that he needed to find work to help out with the family finances. There weren't many jobs available in the city, especially for a young black man with a reform school record. Paige knew, however, that there was one job he could easily get—playing baseball. Paige was certain he had more than enough talent to play professionally.

Leroy's brother, Wilson, nicknamed Paddlefoot, was a pitcher and catcher for a local semiprofessional team, the Mobile Tigers. Leroy challenged the Tigers' coach to face him in batting practice. The coach could not hit a single one of Paige's pitches, and he was hired on the spot.

Paige soon became the Tigers' star player. He perfected the pitching techniques he had learned at the Industrial School, and no one could hit his fastball. At the same time, he began to develop the showmanship for which he would be famous throughout his career. By walking slowly and casually to the mound, he created a sense of suspense before he even threw a single pitch. This was the calm before the storm of his fastball. He also had a way with words and got plenty of

Satchel Paige's first job in baseball was as a pitcher for the
Mobile Tigers, a semiprofessional team in Mobile, Alabama. He
quickly became the team's star player.

laughs from the crowd when he bragged about his pitching and "talked trash" to the other players.

Paige became known as a pitcher who could pull off daring and imaginative stunts. Halfway through the 1926 season, while playing for another semipro team, the Chattanooga Black Lookouts, Paige's teammates committed several errors. The bases were loaded, and the fans booed Paige's team. Sensing that his team was losing fan support, Paige decided to take drastic measures to win back the crowd. He ordered his outfielders to sit down behind the pitching mound. Then, with no one on the diamond in a position to field the ball, Paige struck out the next batter. The crowd, back on his side, cheered wildly, and rumors quickly began to spread about this crazy young pitcher.

In spite of his success, Paige was frustrated because he was not making enough money. Although the Tigers did not like it, Paige would pitch for other teams if they offered him enough money. In addition to pitching, Paige took a job sweeping the stadium of the Mobile Bears, a white minor league team.

The white players had heard about Paige's pitching for the Tigers, and they asked him to give them a demonstration. They were stunned by his skill. After the demonstration, one of the players told him it was too bad he was not white. If he had been white, he would have been able to play in the major leagues. This was the first time Paige had heard these words, but it would not be the last.

Segregation in Baseball

Baseball had not always been segregated. The game was invented in the 1840s, and it became popular during the Civil War. Right after the war, black slaves were set free. Black men were allowed to vote for the first time and some blacks were given positions in local governments. It was during this time that some talented black baseball players also began to play on the same teams as whites.

It didn't take long for things to change, however. Throughout the late nineteenth and early twentieth centuries, Jim Crow laws were established all over the country, particularly in the southern states. These laws created a system of segregation in the United States similar to apartheid in South Africa, where blacks were separated from whites. There were separate schools, hotels, restaurants, water fountains, and rest rooms for whites and blacks. These institutions were supposed to be "separate but equal," but in actuality the institutions for blacks were usually not as high in quality as were the ones for whites.

The Jim Crow laws affected baseball, too. Many white players did not want to continue to play with or against black players. In the 1887–1888 season, the International League, one of the organizations that controlled baseball, changed its rules, formally shutting black players out of white baseball teams.

Suddenly there were no teams on which blacks could play. They had no choice but to set up their own baseball teams and to play against each other. Soon hundreds of such teams were in existence.

Professional Baseball, Separate and Unequal

In the early twentieth century, white baseball was structured pretty much as professional baseball is today. Professional white teams were formally organized into two major leagues, the National League and the American League. Minor league teams would funnel their best young talent up to the major leagues when the players seemed ready to succeed at the next level. There were also semipro teams, in which players had other jobs and only played baseball part-time. Baseball players usually started their careers in the semipro and minor leagues. In many cases, older major league players would end their careers on minor league teams once their skills began to drop off. In this way, their professional baseball careers would come full circle.

With the International League's decision to ban black baseball players from playing on white teams, black players had to struggle to maintain a black baseball culture.

Black baseball was more disorganized and unstable than its white counterpart, particularly in its early years. The terms of a contract were rarely followed. Players often "jumped" or switched teams the minute they were offered more money than they were currently being paid. There were also fewer rules and regulations in black baseball.

Conditions for black players were far worse than those for white players. Black teams usually did not have much money, and they could not hire many relief players. Players often had to stay in the game for the full nine innings even if they were injured. They were generally paid very badly, usually earning about a dollar a game. Sometimes, on bad days, they would only get a pitcher of lemonade in return for their hard

Signs like this one, outside of a Greyhound Bus station in the South, were indicative of the racist attitude African Americans faced during segregation.

work. Also, there was very little money available for equipment. Baseballs were used until they became "mushy," making them very hard to hit.

In addition, the black teams did not own their own stadiums, and they could schedule games in white teams' stadiums only when they were not being used. It was impossible to schedule enough regular games to keep the teams going, so most of them had to barnstorm. This meant that they had to move from town to town like traveling circuses in order to attract enough fans to make ends meet. For these teams, there was no such thing as a home game or hometown fans. Black teams usually traveled in buses, sometimes playing two or three games in different locations within one day. They often had to play in city parks or on playgrounds because actual baseball diamonds were not available. Sometimes, when the town had no hotels or restaurants that would accept black customers, the players had to eat cold sandwiches and sleep on the playing fields.

The Negro Leagues

iven the large number of talented black baseball players who were shut out of the white major leagues, and given the enormous African American fan base, it was only a matter of time before black teams followed the model of the National and American Leagues and became more organized and professional. This new environment allowed Satchel Paige to flourish. He began to make a name for himself even in white sports circles. The Negro leagues would also provide him eventual passage into baseball's promised land—an integrated major league and the National Baseball Hall of Fame.

Andrew "Rube" Foster, a former star pitcher and manager of the Chicago American Giants, founded the Negro National League.

The First Negro National League

Starting in the late 1880s, several attempts were made to organize the black teams into leagues. None were really successful. This was to change in 1920, however, when Andrew "Rube" Foster established the first Negro league.

Foster, a former star pitcher and famous baseball personality, was the manager of the

Chicago American Giants. He had a lot of power in the world of black baseball. Foster felt that if black baseball was more organized, African American teams might eventually be able to play professional championships against white major league teams, thus gaining access to the money and prestige available in the major league world.

Foster asked seven other midwestern teams to join him in establishing the Negro National League. The Negro National League had strict rules, just like the white major leagues, and it fined players, owners, and managers who did not follow these rules. Foster was to play a leading role in this league, and his team, the American Giants, won the League's first three championships.

At first, fans flocked to the Negro National League games. Inspired by the league's profits, other black baseball leagues formed, including the Negro Southern League and the Eastern Colored League. However, all of these leagues ran into problems fairly quickly. Some teams were much better than others, meaning that

Rube Foster's baseball team, the Chicago American Giants, circa 1925

certain teams always won the championships. Generally, the wealthy teams were the ones that dominated the leagues because they could afford the best players and equipment. As in earlier days, players broke the rules of the Negro National League—and their contracts—to switch to the teams that could pay them better. Because there was an imbalance of wealth among teams, the richer teams could lure away talented players. At first, owners tried to maintain some order on their teams, but they were unable to keep it up. Player morale was low due to this inequity and lack of stability.

The strain of keeping his league together began to affect Rube Foster. In 1927, he suffered a mental breakdown and had to be hospitalized. He died a few years later. Once Foster was no longer part of the scene, the Negro league he had established fell apart completely.

First Job in the Negro Leagues

Satchel Paige's career in the Negro leagues was to blossom in this atmosphere of relative chaos. Late in 1926, when Paige was still playing for the Mobile Tigers, a scout for the Chattanooga Black Lookouts came to watch him play. The Black Lookouts were a professional team in the Negro Southern League, and they offered Paige a pitching position. He accepted the job and won almost every game he started for the Chattanooga Black Lookouts.

In 1927, the Chattanooga Black Lookouts traded Paige to the Birmingham Black Barons, the best team in the Negro Southern League. Paige spent the next three years with the Barons. He developed several unique pitches, including the "two-hump blooper" (a changeup), the "Little Tom" (a medium fastball), and the "Long Tom" (a hard fastball).

Things really started happening for Paige in 1929 when the Nashville Elite Giants acquired him. Despite their name, the Giants actually played in Cleveland, Ohio. Playing for them brought Paige to the attention of major league owners and baseball writers who seldom ventured into the South.

The Giants were only one of the many teams that wanted Paige's services. After the regular season ended, Paige continued to play baseball. Because of his growing fame as a pitcher, Paige was tapped to pitch for the Baltimore Black Sox in a series of exhibition games against a white major league team, the Babe Ruth All-Stars. Even though blacks and whites could not play together during the regular professional season, they were free to play exhibition games against each other when the regular season was over. These interracial games were very popular with fans.

To his great disappointment, Paige never got to pitch against the Babe, but he did very well against the rest of Ruth's team, going so far as to strike out twenty-two players in one game. Exhilarated by his success against white players, Paige was eager to take on new challenges.

A New League, A New Team

The late 1920s and early 1930s were a tough period for black teams, which again fell into

Twenty-nine Years of Pitching

Paige played baseball year-round from 1929 to 1958. During this period, he pitched all over North America, in Central America and South America, and in the Caribbean, for all kinds of different teams. He was proud of this achievement. Most players, he said, only lasted ten or fifteen years, playing six months a year. Satchel Paige managed to last twenty-nine years, pitching almost every day.

The legendary Babe Ruth of the New York Yankees

disorganization following the failure of
Foster's Negro National League. In addition,
the Great Depression meant that many fans
were too poor to buy baseball tickets.
However, as soon as the American economy
began to recover from the Depression, people
began to talk about starting up a new Negro
National League.

The first man to succeed at this endeavor was a rich black businessman named Gus Greenlee. Greenlee owned the Pittsburgh Crawfords, one of the best black teams in the country. Hoping that local black fans would buy lots of tickets for his games, Greenlee started the second Negro National League in 1933. This league survived—in one form or another—until 1948.

Greenlee recruited the best players he could find. One of these players was an up-and-coming pitcher from the South . . . Satchel Paige.

Paige was happy to join the Crawfords in 1931. This was the big break he had been hoping for. His new teammates included big Negro league stars like Josh Gibson, Cool Papa Bell, and Judy Johnson. Playing in such company, he knew that real stardom was within his reach.

The Pittsburgh Crawfords

With the formation of the second Negro National League, Satchel Paige began a long but often troubled professional relationship with Gus Greenlee, owner of the Pittsburgh Crawfords. It was while playing for the Crawfords that Paige enjoyed his first real taste of fame and popularity; in other words, the attention of the national press and the American public.

Star Pitcher

Despite all the great players on Gus Greenlee's team, it soon became obvious that Satchel Paige was something special. His "pea ball," or "bee ball" as he liked to call it (because of the way it hummed), was a very powerful fastball that was difficult for batters to see as it went across the plate. Paige put a peculiar wobble on his pitches. Because of the ball's strange motion, hitters couldn't tell what sort of pitch was coming their way. By the time they figured it out, the ball was already in the catcher's hand. Paige's signature windups, like the Model T and the windmill, were fun to watch, as were his stunts on the field. The fans loved him.

Love and Marriage

One night, after Paige led his team to a big victory over the Homestead Grays, Greenlee held a big party in his honor at his restaurant, the Crawford Grill. Paige spied a shy, pretty waitress standing on the other side of the room. Her name was Janet Howard.

Soon, Paige and Janet began to date. Janet didn't like all the traveling that Paige had to do. However, it was necessary for Paige to keep moving around—as he had earlier in his

Dapper, high-rolling Satchel Paige poses by his car.

career—in order to keep pitching for all the teams who wanted him and to make enough money to cover his expenses.

Riding High

Even though he was being paid more money than any of the other players, Paige did not save much of it. He was always running out of cash and asking for advances from Greenlee. Greenlee warned him that he should start saving, but dating Janet only made matters worse. The only money Paige did not spend immediately was the monthly allowance he sent to his mother in Mobile.

In general, Paige was not known for his discipline and seriousness. He was unreliable, and he angered team owners and fans by showing up late or by not showing up at all. Everyone tolerated Paige's behavior, though, because he was such a good pitcher and the Crawfords could not win without him.

In 1934, Paige had one of the best seasons of his career, allowing only 85 hits in 154 innings. As one of the best—and the most popular—pitchers in the Negro leagues, Paige was a shoe-in for a pitching spot on the East team for the second annual East-West All-Star Game. Paige later said that as he was walking out to the mound to start pitching, he heard a fan say, "It's Paige. Good-bye ballgame."

Paige didn't disappoint the fan. He saved the day for his team, allowing only two hits in four innings. This exciting game was one of the first

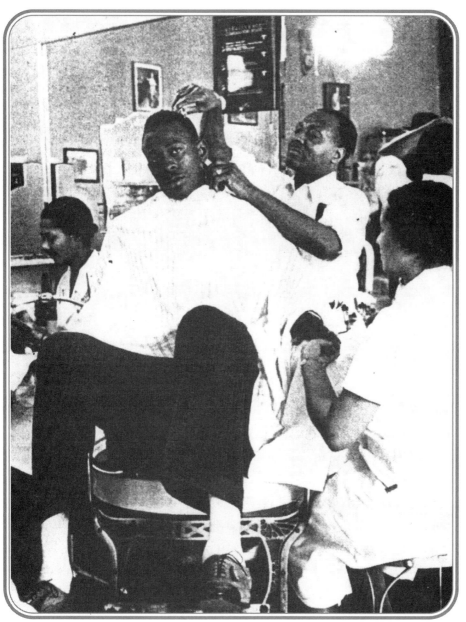

Although Paige made more money than other Negro league players, he was often broke, having squandered much of his salary on grooming and flashy clothes.

Negro league games to be covered by both the black and the white sports press. Some white fans heard about Satchel Paige for the first time.

After Paige's all-star victory, Greenlee was even more eager to hold on to him. He quickly re-signed Paige to a new two-year contract.

Meanwhile, Paige and Janet's relationship took a new turn, and later that year (in 1934), the couple got married. However, Paige began to have serious money problems again. Married life, it turned out, was even more expensive than dating. As usual, he went to Gus Greenlee to ask for an advance. Thinking that he now had Paige locked into a contract, Greenlee refused this latest request for money.

Paige was outraged. He decided to take the first decent job offer he got, and he didn't have to wait long. A few days later, he broke his contract with Greenlee and signed on with the Bismarck Baseball Club, a semipro team in North Dakota. Furious, Greenlee tried to arrange for Paige to be banned from playing on any Negro league team in the future. Paige didn't care. He and Janet packed their bags and left for North Dakota.

Barnstorming

After his split with Gus Greenlee, Satchel Paige entered the world of semipro baseball. Unlike professional baseball, and American society itself, semipro ball was integrated. In this period of barnstorming, Paige would begin to rub elbows with white players, some of whom would become legends of the game. This early experience with integrated play would pave the way for Paige's eventual entry into the major leagues.

Bismarck Baseball Club

The Bismarck Baseball Club was not very good, but it was integrated. This was the first time in Paige's life that he would play on the same team as white players. The team's managers hoped that a talented black pitcher would boost ticket sales to their games, and they were right. Paige won all eighteen of the games he played for the team, and as usual, the fans were crazy about him.

Janet was not too thrilled about the move to North Dakota, especially after she discovered that none of the whites in Bismarck wanted to rent out their houses to a black couple. The newlyweds eventually had to move into an abandoned railway car, the only residence that was available to them.

At first, Paige's white teammates did not like their cocky new pitcher very much. During one game, after Paige yelled at them for missing a few routine fly balls, his outfielders rebelled. They refused to go out to field when a new inning started. The fans cheered, thinking the whole thing was a stunt like the one Paige had pulled back in Mobile when he had ordered his outfield to sit down behind the pitching mound. Paige had to apologize before the outfielders would take their positions again.

A Sioux Indian camp. Satchel Paige developed friendships with Sioux Indians on a reservation near Bismarck.

The only people in Bismarck with whom Paige really felt comfortable were the Sioux Indians. He visited them often on their reservation outside the city. Paige liked to tell the story of the day he visited an elderly Sioux man who raised rattlesnakes. The man gave Paige a special ointment to use as an antidote whenever he was bitten by the snakes. For the rest of his life, Paige claimed to use the ointment as a salve for his pitching arm and he credited it with contributing to his longevity as a pitcher.

Barnstorming with Major Leaguers

When the season in Bismarck ended, Paige and Janet left North Dakota. Janet went back to Pittsburgh alone, while Paige formed a team of his own, the Satchel Paige All-Stars. Paige had enjoyed barnstorming against the Babe Ruth All-Stars back in 1929, and he wanted to repeat the experience with other white major league teams. There was no shortage of potential opponents.

Major leaguers welcomed the opportunity to make some extra money on off-season exhibition games, and they were especially eager to try their luck at hitting Paige's famous fastball, an opportunity they were denied during the baseball season because of segregation.

There were some differences in style between white major leaguers and the black players they played against in these exhibition games. By the 1930s, the major leagues had outlawed tampering with the ball and other practices of the old style of baseball play that was still legal in the Negro leagues.

Another difference was that black players were often forced to be as skilled at entertainment as they were at baseball. During this time, because popular movies and radio shows portrayed blacks as lovable clowns, managers of black teams hoped that more white fans would come to the games if their players performed amusing stunts. Also, when barnstorming black teams played white teams, jokes helped to smooth ruffled feathers and soothe offended sensibilities when the black teams won.

The challenge for black players was to ensure that even when they were forced to clown around, they kept playing good baseball. Satchel Paige was a master at maintaining this balance. It was because of this that he was so popular on the barnstorming circuit. People wanted excitement and entertainment at barnstorming games, and nobody could deliver both better than Paige.

Even if Paige and his All-Stars joked around on the field, they insisted on being treated with respect. While he was barnstorming, Paige always refused to play in towns that would not let blacks sleep in their hotels.

While playing for the Kansas City Monarchs, Satchel Paige delivers a pitch during a barnstorming game against the New York Cuban Stars at New York's Yankee Stadium on August 2, 1942.

Cannibals and Clowns

Some black teams, like the Zulu Cannibal Giants, the Miami Clowns (later the Ethiopian Clowns), and the Indianapolis Clowns, took entertaining the fans to an extreme. They would go so far as to paint their faces, wear grass skirts like African tribes, bat with large wooden war clubs, perform comedy routines before and during games, and adopt player names like "Impo" and "Limpopo." The actual game that was played became less important than the costume spectacle on the field, which was designed to appeal to the racist attitudes of white fans.

Dizzy Dean and Joe DiMaggio

One of the Satchel Paige All-Stars' barnstorming rivals was a team led by the major league pitcher Dizzy Dean. Dizzy and Paige had a lot in common. Dizzy liked to throw fastballs, and he was an uneducated, though slick and entertaining, showman from the South, just like Paige.

The two pitchers had a friendly but competitive relationship. Of the six games they played against each other in one tournament, Paige won four, and Dizzy had to admit that

While pitching for the Satchel Paige All-Stars, Paige (*left*),
formed a friendly rivalry with major league pitcher Dizzy Dean.

Paige was a better pitcher than he was. Years later, Dizzy wrote in an article that skinny old Satchel Paige, with his long arms and odd windup and delivery, was the best pitcher he had ever seen. "If Satch and I was pitching on the same team," he once claimed, "we'd clinch the pennant by the Fourth of July and go fishing until World Series time."

Dizzy Dean wasn't the only famous white player Paige pitched against during this period of his career. In one memorable exhibition game, Paige struggled to prevent Dick Bartell's All-Stars from defeating his own team, which consisted of himself, another Negro leaguer, and an assortment of inexperienced semipro players. Paige struck out as many of his opponents as he could and did his best to hit the ball whenever he was at bat. He even coached his inexperienced teammates from first base when he wasn't actually playing.

Despite his best efforts, however, an umpire called Paige out late in the game. Paige was rattled by this rare failure. In the next inning,

Joe DiMaggio, who was about to move to New York to begin his legendary career with the Yankees, hit one of Paige's pitches, resulting in the winning home run. After the game, Paige heard DiMaggio say that he knew that he could make it with the Yankees now, after finally getting a hit off "Ol' Satch." DiMaggio also went on the record as saying that Paige was "the best and fastest pitcher I've ever faced."

Dreaming of the Major Leagues

Paige's spectacular performance against white major leaguers impressed sports journalists. Some of them even wrote about what a shame it was that great players like him were barred from the major leagues because of the color of their skin.

Paige pretended he was perfectly happy where he was, but in actuality, he was hoping to be asked to try out for the majors. He was flattered by the compliments he was getting from famous white players like Dizzy Dean, and he couldn't help resenting the fact that he wasn't allowed to

Dangerous Fastballs

Satchel Paige is said to be the reason that baseball players wear plastic helmets today. For a 1936 barnstorming game, a white team from Borger, Texas, wore helmets around their caps so that they wouldn't get hurt if one of Satchel's fastballs hit them in the head. It was the first time any baseball player had worn protection on his head.

play with them all the time. He wanted the money and prestige that were available in the major leagues *and* the social acceptance of blacks that integrated play would represent.

Satchel Paige also wanted to prove that he could strike out white major leaguers under any circumstances. It was easier to strike out major leaguers in off-season exhibition games—when they were tired and out of shape—than it was to strike them out during the season,when they were at the top of their game and were chasing the championship. Until he pitched in the majors, Paige wouldn't be able to prove to the world that he really was the best pitcher around.

The End of the Road?

The attention Paige was getting from the world of white baseball made Greenlee change his mind about banning Paige from the Negro leagues, and he soon asked Paige to come back to the Crawfords. At the same time, Greenlee put pressure on other Negro league teams to refuse to hire him, limiting Paige's ability to sign up with other teams. Paige felt that he had no choice but to agree to pitch for the Crawfords during the 1936 season.

Playing for High Stakes in the Dominican Republic

Despite Greenlee's renewed attempts to lock him in, Paige didn't stay with the Crawfords

Rafael Trujillo *(center)* **poses with his team, Los Dragones.**
Satchel Paige joined the team for a brief stint in 1937.

for long. In 1937, at spring training in New
Orleans, he was approached by two agents of
the president of the Dominican Republic,
Rafael Trujillo. Baseball was and continues to
be extremely popular in the Caribbean and in
Latin America, and local politicians used
baseball teams to build popularity with their
constituents. Trujillo was facing a strong

challenge from another political party and was looking for an opportunity to polish his image. He wanted to make sure his baseball team, Los Dragones, was the best in the country, and he was willing to spend a lot of money to do it. One of the players he most wanted to recruit was Satchel Paige.

Paige had a pretty good deal with the Crawfords, but the two Dominican men made him an offer he couldn't refuse. For what amounted to $9,000 for a few weeks of work— more money than he'd ever been paid before— he agreed to sign on with Trujillo's team.

Miseries in Mexico

Back in the United States after his brief stint with Los Dragones, Paige discovered that once again, Greenlee had forgiven him for breaking his contract, and he went back to pitching for the Crawfords. Over the summer, Paige barnstormed against another famous

Satchel Paige *(right)* and owner Gus Greenlee *(left)* shared a
long-standing, if sometimes troubled, professional relationship.

white pitcher, Bob Feller, and traveled around for a while with a team from the House of David, a fundamentalist religious group.

In 1938, Paige broke his Crawfords contract again and went to play for a baseball team in Mexico. Greenlee's patience was finally exhausted; he traded Paige to the Newark Eagles. Paige decided to stay in Mexico, however, and he never played for the Eagles. Unfortunately, Mexico was to prove bad for Paige's health.

Throughout his career, Paige had been careful to treat his pitching arm well. He never pitched without loosening up first. He always wore thick, long-sleeved shirts on the mound, and he took hot baths before games so that he would never be cold and stiff. He also claimed to frequently use his Sioux snake ointment, which seemed to soothe and loosen his weary, aging muscles. Paige thought his arm would last forever, even though he used it practically every day. That summer in Mexico, however, he was proven wrong.

Bearded Baseball Players

The House of David was a religious order that demanded that all its male converts grow beards. The order's baseball team helped to spread the word about its beliefs. Paige could only grow a mustache, so his teammates lent him a long, red false beard. He got very upset one day when his arm got tangled up in the beard, causing an important pitch to go awry.

One day, he began to feel an ache in his arm, but he kept pitching because he was being paid by the game and didn't want to lose any money. The pain didn't go away, and his manager finally told him to take the afternoon off. Paige had a few drinks of tequila and went to bed. When he got up the next morning, he couldn't lift his arm. He rushed to the ballpark and tried to throw a few pitches. To his horror, he realized he could not throw a ball farther than a few feet.

The team's manager called in some doctors, but no one could figure out what was wrong with Paige's arm. After a few days, he was sent home. But the American doctors couldn't help him either. One even told him that he would never pitch again.

A Sudden Downfall

Paige couldn't believe what had happened. Just a few weeks earlier, everyone had wanted to hire him. But now, with his pitching arm gone, no one was interested in him. He was still only about thirty-two years old, and he could have managed a baseball team or become a coach. However, Paige's years of breaking contracts and failing to show up for games came back to haunt him. His old contacts in the Negro leagues did not feel like doing him any favors.

Depressed and lonely, Paige couldn't bring himself to go back to Janet. He felt like a failure. And not only that, he was experiencing money problems again, this time with no hope of finding a quick solution in terms of getting a new job. The man who used to have his pick of job offers in the United States and beyond suddenly found that his phone had stopped ringing. With no savings or prospects, he had to pawn his belongings, including his fancy car and fishing equipment, just to survive.

A New Start

ollowing his mysterious arm injury, it looked like the end of the road for Satchel Paige. Yet this period would turn out to be only a brief lull in a baseball career that still had plenty of kick left in it. Paige would come out of this dark time with a new kind of pitch, a new team, a new love, and a new round of national publicity. Far from having reached the end of the road, Paige found himself poised for a new level of success and recognition.

Saved

Just when he was losing hope, Paige got a call from J. L. Wilkinson, the owner of the Kansas City Monarchs. The Monarchs were the best

black team in the Midwest, and Wilkinson was
the kind of owner who looked out for players
who were going through a streak of bad luck or
were nearing the end of their careers.

Since Paige could not really pitch, Wilkinson
gave him a spot on one of the Monarchs'

Though Paige's pitching with the Monarchs got off to a rough start
due to an arm injury, he soon became the team's star pitcher.

traveling teams. He began to barnstorm with them. It was an embarrassing time for Paige. Fans came to the games, expecting to see the old, spectacular Satchel Paige. They weren't impressed with what he had turned into since his arm injury. He even overheard one boy ask his dad how he had ever gotten anyone out.

For a few months, Paige took it easy, pitching a couple of innings here and there. Then one day, he was throwing a few warm-up pitches. All of a sudden, his arm stopped hurting. He called his catcher and told him to get ready to catch a fastball—the first he'd thrown since his injury. It sailed into the catcher's glove with speed and power.

Paige's arm was back. Jubilant, he called Wilkinson with the news that very evening. The owner told him that he could join the Monarchs for the 1939 season.

Back on Top

Soon Paige was at the top of his game. Because the Kansas City Monarchs were one of the first teams to play night baseball, using portable spotlights that they took with them from town to town, Paige sometimes had to play three games in one day. Even though he was pitching more than ever, it was as if nothing had ever happened to his arm. He led the Monarchs to four straight Negro American League championship victories in the early forties.

In one legendary game in 1942, the Monarchs faced the Homestead Grays. Paige loved to tell the story of what happened when he faced his old teammate, Josh Gibson, in this game. Paige had always wanted to prove that he was a better pitcher than Gibson was a hitter, and he made a $5 bet with Gibson that he would be able to strike him out.

By the seventh inning of the game, however, Paige had not yet succeeded in his mission. He decided to take drastic and risky measures to ensure that he won the bet. There were two outs and two batters up before Gibson's turn at bat, so Paige decided to deliberately walk the two batters. His teammates thought he was crazy, because if Gibson hit a home run, the Grays would win the game. Nevertheless, Paige insisted. Gibson came up to the plate. Amazingly, before each pitch, Paige told Gibson what kind of ball he was going to throw. He then pitched the ball, and Gibson missed it—three times in a row. The fans went wild. Paige had psyched Gibson out to win both his bet and the ball game.

During this phase of his career, Paige developed his famous "hesitation" pitch. He knew that his fastball wasn't quite as powerful as it had been before his injury, and he was getting older. Because of this, he decided he needed something extra to ensure that batters would keep missing his pitches. What Paige came up with was to begin putting his foot down before throwing the ball—making it look like he had already thrown it. Players would swing for the ball while Paige was still holding it in his hand.

Paige's experiences after his injury made him more careful about breaking contracts, and he did not want to treat Wilkinson badly. He wound up playing for the Monarchs, on and off, for the next eight years. Wilkinson also lent him

out occasionally, and Paige continued to play
for other teams off-season.

A New Woman in Paige's Life

Following his divorce from Janet in 1943, Paige
returned to Kansas City where, one day, he
decided to go shopping in a drugstore. An
attractive woman rang up his purchase. She
didn't know who Paige was, and because his
pride was hurt, he found an excuse to complain
to the manager about her.

Later, Paige felt guilty about his rude
behavior. He went back to the store again and
again, each time asking to be served by the
"half-smart girl," Lahoma Brown. Eventually,
when it seemed like she had forgiven him,
Paige asked her out to dinner. It was the
beginning of a relationship that would last for
the rest of Paige's life. Later, in his
autobiography, Paige described Lahoma as the
only woman who had ever been able to make
him slow down and settle down.

Although his first marriage ended in divorce, Satchel Paige found true love with his second wife, Lahoma Brown.

A few years after his divorce from Janet was finalized, Satchel Paige and Lahoma married. They eventually had eight children together.

Growing Celebrity

Time, *Life* magazine, and the *Saturday Evening Post* all published profiles of Paige around this time. Although the profiles praised Paige's masterful pitching, they also stereotyped him as a crazy clown, a buffoonish entertainer, and an exotic witchdoctor. Much was made of the mystery of his age, his diet, his snake oil, and his fancy clothes.

In later years, Paige complained about the way these journalists made him look and sound

Paige's new celebrity status and matching salary afforded him luxuries—such as this plane—that were unheard of for professional athletes at that time.

peculiar. But at the time, he didn't try hard to convince them otherwise. The articles that were written about him made him into a household name all over the United States. And Paige knew that the more famous he was, the more money would come his way.

He was right. All the publicity Paige was receiving attracted more fans to baseball, and the Negro league managers rewarded him accordingly. His salary was almost $40,000 a year, making him the highest-paid athlete in the world at the time. Wilkinson even bought Paige his own private plane to take him from game to game.

Fear of Flying

Satchel Paige was probably the first pitcher ever to be given a personal plane by his team, but he didn't really appreciate the privilege. During his first flight, his small plane was caught in a storm, and he refused to fly in it again. The pilot told him that if he missed the game the next day, he wouldn't get the $500 that he had been promised. Always reluctant to lose money, Paige agreed to try a second flight. This time, the plane sprung an oil leak. Paige was terrified that it would drop out of the sky. After the plane landed, he swore he would never board it again, and this time he meant it. The Monarchs ended up selling the plane.

Integration

atchel Paige's career was back on track, and he was enjoying all of the accompanying success and publicity. Elsewhere in the world, however, the storm clouds of war were gathering. As dark a time as this was for the United States, World War II indirectly led to a development that many baseball players and fans had long wished for but rarely had believed possible: integration of the game. Though Paige would not be the first black player admitted to the major leagues, he would eventually benefit from the courageous trailblazing of Jackie Robinson and the Brooklyn Dodgers' owner, Branch Rickey. More than twenty years after becoming a professional

Jackie Robinson *(second from right)* signed with the Brooklyn Dodgers, becoming the first black baseball player to play for the major leagues and paving the way for Satchel Paige.

baseball player, Paige would finally gain his long-deserved place in the major leagues.

Jackie Robinson

The United States entered World War II in 1942, and many baseball players left to enlist in the armed forces. More than ever, the majors needed players of Paige's quality.

Rumors began to circulate that Branch Rickey, the owner of the Brooklyn Dodgers, was planning to integrate his team. In October 1945, the news broke that Rickey had assigned a black player to the Montreal Royals, a minor league farm team for the Brooklyn Dodgers. The black player was Jackie Robinson, one of Paige's former teammates from the Monarchs.

Rickey had chosen the first black player carefully. Everyone would be watching this man and looking for flaws. Robinson would have to put up with insults and abuse from racists who wanted to see him fail. Rickey wanted someone who could withstand the pressure. He also needed someone who would follow the rules and not embarrass him off the field. Robinson fit the bill in a way that Paige did not. He was young and college educated, a good all-around athlete. Robinson wasn't the best African American player, but he was very good. He was dignified, reserved, and dependable. He was a family man, and he didn't drink or stay out all night.

Paige, with his reputation for clowning, unreliability, and greed, was not the kind of man Rickey was looking for. Still, Paige was upset at the news about Robinson. Paige knew he was getting older and was not as good a pitcher as he used to be, but somehow he had still expected to be the first black player to break the color barrier.

Robinson played well, and in 1947, he was called up to the Dodgers. The experiment of introducing a black player into the majors was declared a success. More major league teams began to sign African American players. However, once again, Paige's phone was not ringing.

Cleveland Indians

In 1948, it was finally Paige's turn. Paige had a good relationship with Bill Veeck, the owner of the Cleveland Indians, a major league team. Veeck had wanted to hire Paige ever since he had seen him pitch in the early 1930s, and he had considered signing him right after Robinson joined the Dodgers. But, since Paige was getting older, Veeck was afraid people would see the hire as a publicity stunt.

Veeck changed his mind about hiring Paige when the Indians found themselves in need of a great pitcher to help them win the American League pennant. Veeck's scouts told him that Paige was still the best pitcher in the Negro leagues. Veeck organized a tryout for Paige at the Indians' ballpark, and Paige passed the test with flying colors.

Satchel Paige is shown here pitching for the New York Black Yankees. He was later named major league baseball's Rookie of the Year in 1948 after his first year with the Cleveland Indians.

Paige knew that he might have lost some of his power, but he still had the moves to outsmart most batters. Also, he was very nervous. At his first major league game against the St. Louis Browns, 35,000 fans came out to see the famous rookie pitch, and the pressure on Paige was enormous. When he was called to the mound, photographers rushed out onto the field to get pictures of him. Paige's stomach was acting up, and at first he was very stiff. But soon he loosened up, and he didn't allow any runs before he was taken out of the game.

Paige suffered a blow when umpires banned one of his most powerful weapons, the hesitation pitch, a pitch that allowed him to compensate for his previously injured arm and slowing fastball. Nevertheless, in the games that followed, he managed a couple of shutouts and won six games out of seven, helping the Indians win the American League pennant and get into their first World Series in twenty-eight years. His earned run average (ERA) that season was 2.48, and he struck out enough batters to be named Rookie of the Year, an honor usually associated with youth and inexperience. This "rookie" was in his forties and had played professional baseball for more than twenty years!

Paige didn't let the pressures of the major leagues change him too much. He continued to enjoy life. He refused to exercise, he drank too much, and he frequently stayed out late. He also showed up late or missed games, just as he had in the Negro leagues. But Lou Boudreau, the Indians' manager, was not as tolerant as the Negro

Cleveland Indians manager Lou Boudreau *(left)* leads a parade in celebration of his team's World Series victory in Cleveland, Ohio, on October 12, 1948.

league managers had been. He fined Paige for his rule breaking and allowed him to pitch in fewer and fewer games.

The situation was so bad that it didn't look like Boudreau would let Paige play in the 1948 World Series. Paige sat through the first few games of the series, itching to pitch, but Boudreau ignored him. In the fifth game, however, Boudreau had no choice. He went through all the other pitchers on his bench before he finally called Paige to the mound, much to the delight of the crowd. Hassled by the umpires for his unorthodox pitching style, Paige only pitched for two-thirds of an inning before he was taken out of the game. But that was enough to make him officially the first black pitcher to play in a major league World Series.

The Indians won the World Series that year, but things didn't improve for Paige. His stomach hurt, his legs ached, and he had to have all of his teeth removed. Boudreau decided that Paige was no longer of much use to the team, and in 1950 he was fired.

Decline and a Final Blaze of Glory

Although African Americans were slowly beginning to enter the major leagues, the flip side to this landmark achievement was the decline and eventual disappearance of the Negro leagues. Just as the black teams were beginning to disappear—made irrelevant by the integration of baseball—so too did Paige.

Paige's career begin to wind down as his skills deteriorated. Yet this was not a sad time for Paige. Even though his age was finally catching up with him, new opportunities presented themselves in coaching, in publishing, and even in Hollywood. The most valuable opportunity offered to Paige, however, was the chance to go out on top, leaving baseball in a final blaze of glory.

Empty bleachers became a common sight as Negro league baseball lost talented players to the major leagues.

The Decline of Negro Leagues

When the Kansas City Monarchs heard that Paige was a free agent again, they were eager to sign him. Unfortunately, the Monarchs and other black teams were caught in a downward spiral. Integration of the major leagues had been very bad for the Negro leagues. As black players broke their contracts to go to the majors, Negro league teams lost their best players. Promising young players began to go straight from high school to minor league farm teams, not stopping to play in the Negro leagues. But the worst problem was that the fans started to lose interest in the Negro leagues. All the action was switching to the majors.

By the end of the 1940s, most Negro league teams were forced to cut player salaries. Many talented black players who were not able to get into the majors had to play out the rest of their careers outside the United States. The few Negro league teams that did survive into the 1950s and 1960s had to resort to publicity stunts like hiring midgets, clowns, and women to play for them. Given that the black teams were being raided for talent by the major leagues, Paige hoped that someone would invite him back to the majors soon.

Back to the Majors

In 1951, Bill Veeck bought a new major league team, the St. Louis Browns, and asked Paige to pitch for it. Paige did not care that the Browns were in last place in their league. He was happy to be in the majors again. He also liked most of his teammates, who respected him and often asked him for advice.

St. Louis Browns' owner, Bill Veeck, looks on as Satchel Paige signs his third contract with the team on January 10, 1953.

Roger Hornsby, the Browns' manager, was tough: He treated his players like new recruits in the army. He forced Paige to take part in team practices, to run laps, and to arrive on time. Paige did not enjoy this strictness at all, but he had to admit that the hard work did him good on the pitching mound. His record was so good that he became the best relief pitcher in baseball that year. He was named to the American League All-Star team in 1952 and 1953, the first African American player to achieve this honor.

Unfortunately, it soon became apparent that Paige's pitching wasn't really strong enough to face major league hitters anymore. His worst year ever came in 1953. When the Browns moved to Baltimore to become the Orioles, his second major league team took the opportunity to let him go.

Paige still wasn't ready to give up pitching. From 1954 to 1956, he continued to barnstorm and play for the Monarchs. Then, in 1956, he got yet another call from Veeck.

Pride in His Race

Over the years, Paige had become less willing to put up with people who treated him badly because of his skin color. Once, a hotel clerk refused to check him into the same hotel with his Browns teammates. Paige went to the airport and took the next plane out of town. His manager called him and begged him to return. Only after Paige got an apology from the hotel did he agree to come back.

The call was about a pitching position with the Miami Marlins. Even though Paige's pitching skills had lessened, he continued to be extremely popular with the fans. Some people said that Veeck was using the old pitcher to get laughs. For Paige's first appearance, Veeck hired a helicopter to drop him off on the baseball field. A rocking chair was set up in the bullpen for Paige to sit in when he wasn't on the mound. The fans really loved these antics, and attendance at the Marlin games was high.

In his first year with the Marlins, Paige proved the critics wrong by pitching well.

But after Veeck left the team, Paige couldn't get along with the new owners, especially after they lowered his salary. Then they added insult to injury by putting him on the inactive list for several months, and by refusing to pay him at all.

Paige desperately wanted to leave the Marlins, but he didn't know how else he would make a living. At fifty-five, he felt he was getting too old to barnstorm, but he had to work. Since he had only played in the majors for a few years, he didn't qualify for the minimum baseball pension of $250 a month, and as usual he didn't have any money in the bank.

Paige's Acting Debut

Then, in September 1958, an exciting offer came Paige's way. Some Hollywood producers wanted him to play the role of a black cavalry officer in *The Wonderful Country*, a cowboy movie starring Robert Mitchum. Paige and his family were thrilled. The movie was being shot in Mexico, and Lahoma and the kids packed their bags to join Paige on the set.

Satchel Paige, on the set of the 1958 western film *The Wonderful Country*, where he made his acting debut as a black cavalry sergeant alongside Hollywood legend Robert Mitchum.

Paige soon got the hang of acting; he learned to ride a horse and cry for the camera. He told a reporter that he liked the movies because he got to sit down a lot. He also liked the generous pay. If anyone in Hollywood showed any interest in him as an actor, he would be happy to leave baseball behind and embark on a new career as a movie star.

Swan Song

Unfortunately, no more movie offers came Paige's way. For the next six years, he had to continue to pitch for a variety of minor league teams, including the Indianapolis Clowns, the Harlem Globetrotters, and the Portland Beavers. The aging pitcher traveled around in old buses or in his station wagon, staying at a different hotel every night.

Paige also found time during this period to write his autobiography, *Maybe I'll Pitch Forever*. Published in 1962, it was filled with both humorous and poignant stories about Paige's life. Paige's version of what had happened in the past often differed from what other people had to say about the same events. The book was very successful and is still in print today.

On September 25, 1965, Paige made his final appearance in a major league game.

A publicity-hungry owner, Charles O. Finley, asked the fifty-nine-year-old Paige to pitch one game for his team, the Kansas City Athletics. Many people thought this stunt would be an embarrassment for Paige, and he himself doubted his ability to hold his own against hitters who were forty years younger. But for a paycheck of $5,000, Paige was willing to give it a shot. It turned out to be a triumphant evening for him. In the course of three innings, Paige allowed only one hit, and he struck out seven batters in a row.

How to Stay Young

Paige had a talent for coming up with witty, memorable sayings. A journalist once asked him how he stayed so young, and this was the advice he gave:

- Avoid fried meats which angry up the blood.
- If your stomach disputes you, lie down and pacify it with cool thoughts.
- Keep the juices flowing by jangling around gently as you move.
- Go very light on the vices, such as carrying on in society—the social ramble ain't restful.
- Avoid running at all times.
- And don't look back. Something might be gaining on you.

Twilight of a Legend

inally, after almost forty years in baseball, Satchel Paige's career was coming to an end. What followed his retirement was a long period of stability, honors, and respect—things to which Paige was not accustomed. His post-baseball life included a series of public appearances and celebrity endorsements. During these years, Paige also reached the pinnacle of his career—being inducted into the National Baseball Hall of Fame.

The Road to Retirement

After Paige's performance in the Kansas City Athletics game in 1965, owner Charles O.

Satchel Paige, Atlanta Braves assistant trainer and pitching coach, hops over a row of bats during his daily workout.

Finley said that he might hire Paige as a pitching coach. Paige needed just 158 more days in the majors to qualify for a pension. But the offer did not come through, and Paige had to keep pitching wherever he could.

In 1968, the Atlanta Braves hired Paige as a pitching coach. The team's owner said that he wanted to make sure Paige qualified for the pension he needed. Paige stayed with the Braves until the required 158 days had passed. He officially retired in 1969, at the age of sixty-three.

The Hall of Fame

In the 1950s and 1960s, during the civil rights era, African Americans and other minorities began to demand equal rights with whites in American society. As a result, many people turned their attention to segregation in the National Baseball Hall of Fame in Cooperstown, New York. Perhaps the greatest honor that a baseball player can receive is to be voted into the Hall of Fame, but until 1962, when Jackie Robinson was inducted, no black players were enshrined there.

After Paige's retirement in 1969, the Baseball Writers Association of America started a campaign to admit him and other Negro leaguers into the Hall of Fame. Bill Veeck, Dizzy Dean, Bob Feller, Ted Williams, and others came forward to say how much Paige, in particular, deserved the honor.

A proud Satchel Paige stands by his plaque in the Baseball Hall of Fame on August 9, 1971, the day of his induction.

Finally, in 1971, the Hall of Fame officials agreed to admit stars of the pre-1947 Negro leagues. They set up a committee to pick one player from the Negro leagues every year. Satchel Paige was the committee's first choice.

August 9, 1971, the day on which Paige was inducted into the Hall of Fame, was one of the proudest of his life. In his usual style, he gave an entertaining speech at the awards ceremony. He contrasted the praise he was receiving that day with all the bad names the players who were already inside the Hall of Fame had called him. He then remarked that baseball had turned him from a second-class citizen into a second-class immortal.

The Final Years

Paige spent the last ten years of his life living off his celebrity. He settled down with his family in Kansas City, where he spent most of his days out on the town, visiting friends and telling stories in bars. He was hired to promote a minor league team, the Tulsa Oilers. He was inducted into the Missouri Sports Hall of Fame. A TV movie, *Don't Look Back: The Satchel Paige Story*, was made about his life, and he served as a consultant on it. Louis Gossett Jr. played the role of Paige.

In the early 1980s, Paige developed terminal emphysema combined with heart problems. He was confined to a wheelchair and he had to have an oxygen tank with him at all times.

Satchel Paige *(second from left)* entertains admirers in a bar and grill owned by Gus Greenlee, Paige's longtime associate and the former manager of the Pittsburgh Crawfords.

On June 5th, 1982, Paige made his final public appearance. The Kansas City government had cleaned up an abandoned baseball field and had named it for him. Paige was deeply touched.

A few days later, on June 8, Paige sent Lahoma, his wife of thirty-five years, to the pharmacy to get some medicine to relieve his chest pains. When she came back, Satchel Paige was dead. He died of a heart attack.

Paige's funeral was held on June 12. There were many celebrities among the 150 mourners. Speeches were made and articles were written in Paige's honor. Even in death, Paige kept an air of mystery about him. The inscription on his headstone gave his birthdate as "?".

Having earned his place in the pantheon of baseball greats, Satchel Paige spent his final years as a celebrity sports figure.

Satchel Paige's Legacy

Satchel Paige was acknowledged as a skilled pitcher, but he was also criticized throughout his career. Some people disliked the way he clowned on the field, lived a wild life, and jumped to a new team every time he was offered a fatter paycheck.

However, no one could deny that Paige had made enormous contributions to Negro league baseball. Some argue that he even saved it, especially during the Depression. The press made him into a legend, on a par with white stars such as Joe DiMaggio. Paige traveled more than anyone else, exposing fans to excellence in black baseball. He helped his teams set attendance records and was often their biggest draw. If he had not been a skilled entertainer, he would not have been able to attract the kind of attention that he did, especially from white fans. And if white fans had not noticed the talented players in black baseball, it probably would have taken a lot longer for African

American players to be integrated into the major leagues.

Statistics were not regularly kept in Negro league games, so there is no official record of many of Satchel Paige's stunning achievements. But it has been estimated that he played in about 2,500 games. He claimed to have won

Jackie Robinson's widow, Rachel Robinson, stands before a statue of Satchel Paige at the Negro Leagues Baseball Museum in Kansas City, Missouri.

2,000 games, 300 of them shutouts, while pitching for 250 different teams. He is said to have recorded 64 consecutive scoreless innings, a stretch of 21 straight wins, and a 31–4 record in 1933. In Bismarck, North Dakota, he started 29 games in one month (present-day pitchers may start roughly eight games a month at most). In his 179 major league games, Paige did not commit a single error. At the age of forty-two, Paige became the oldest rookie in baseball, winning six of his seven contests and helping the Cleveland Indians to a pennant and a World Series appearance against the Boston Braves. In 1952, at age forty-six, Paige won 12 games with the St. Louis Browns and became the oldest player ever to be selected to the all-star team.

This impressive record, combined with his unique brand of showmanship, makes it easy to agree with Paige that he may indeed have been the "World's Greatest Pitcher." He was certainly one of the most memorable pitchers the world has ever seen.

Timeline

July 7, 1906 The date on which Leroy "Satchel" Paige may have been born, in Mobile, Alabama. Neither Paige nor his mother was sure what day or year he was actually born, but a birth certificate for a Leroy Page born on this day is filed in the city of Mobile. A childhood friend claimed that Paige was born in 1900.

1918 Paige is caught shoplifting and is sent to the Industrial School for Negro Children, a reform school, in Mount Meigs, Alabama. It is here that he received an education and developed the pitching skills that eventually carried him to the National Baseball Hall of Fame.

1923 Paige is released from the Industrial School and returns to Mobile.

1924 Paige becomes the star player of the Mobile Tigers, a semiprofessional

team. With the Tigers he would
perfect the pitching techniques he
learned at the Industrial School and
begin to develop his trademark crowd-
pleasing showmanship.

May 1, 1926 Paige makes his
professional baseball debut in the
Negro Southern League, pitching for
the Chattanooga Black Lookouts in a
5–4 victory over the Birmingham
Black Barons.

1927 The Chattanooga Black Lookouts
trade Paige to the Birmingham Black
Barons, the best team in the Negro
Southern League. He played for the
Barons for the next three years.

1929 The Nashville Elite Giants acquire
Paige from Birmingham.

1931 Paige joins the Pittsburgh
Crawfords, one of the teams in the
newly formed Negro National
League. His teammates included
other famous Negro League
Hall of Famers, such as Josh

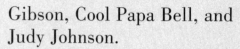

Gibson, Cool Papa Bell, and
Judy Johnson.

July 4, 1934 Paige pitches a no-hitter
against the Homestead Grays in
Pittsburgh. After the game, he drives to
Chicago and shuts out the Chicago
American Giants later the same day.
Paige pitches two shutouts in two
different cities in one day!

1934 Following one of the best seasons
of his career, in which he allowed
only 85 hits in 154 innings, Paige
earns a spot in the East-West All-Star
Game and pitches the East team to
victory. Later this year he marries
Janet Howard, breaks his contract
with the Crawfords, and signs up with
the Bismarck Baseball Club, a
semiprofessional barnstorming team
in North Dakota.

1936 Paige returns to the Pittsburgh
Crawfords.

1937 Paige plays for a Dominican
Republic team, Los Dragones. He soon
returns to the Crawfords.

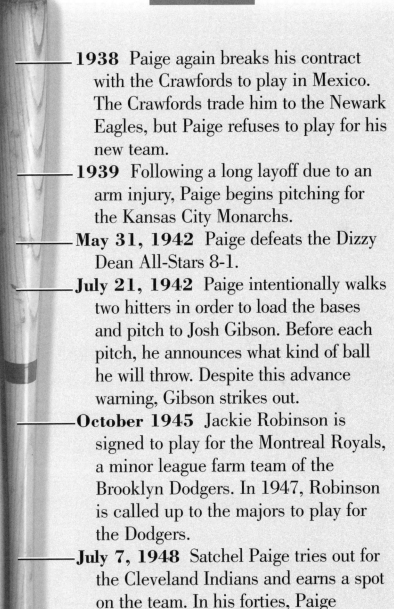

1938 Paige again breaks his contract with the Crawfords to play in Mexico. The Crawfords trade him to the Newark Eagles, but Paige refuses to play for his new team.

1939 Following a long layoff due to an arm injury, Paige begins pitching for the Kansas City Monarchs.

May 31, 1942 Paige defeats the Dizzy Dean All-Stars 8-1.

July 21, 1942 Paige intentionally walks two hitters in order to load the bases and pitch to Josh Gibson. Before each pitch, he announces what kind of ball he will throw. Despite this advance warning, Gibson strikes out.

October 1945 Jackie Robinson is signed to play for the Montreal Royals, a minor league farm team of the Brooklyn Dodgers. In 1947, Robinson is called up to the majors to play for the Dodgers.

July 7, 1948 Satchel Paige tries out for the Cleveland Indians and earns a spot on the team. In his forties, Paige

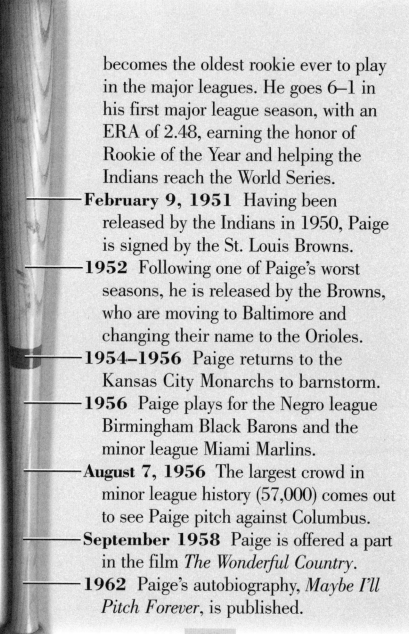

becomes the oldest rookie ever to play in the major leagues. He goes 6–1 in his first major league season, with an ERA of 2.48, earning the honor of Rookie of the Year and helping the Indians reach the World Series.

February 9, 1951 Having been released by the Indians in 1950, Paige is signed by the St. Louis Browns.

1952 Following one of Paige's worst seasons, he is released by the Browns, who are moving to Baltimore and changing their name to the Orioles.

1954–1956 Paige returns to the Kansas City Monarchs to barnstorm.

1956 Paige plays for the Negro league Birmingham Black Barons and the minor league Miami Marlins.

August 7, 1956 The largest crowd in minor league history (57,000) comes out to see Paige pitch against Columbus.

September 1958 Paige is offered a part in the film *The Wonderful Country*.

1962 Paige's autobiography, *Maybe I'll Pitch Forever*, is published.

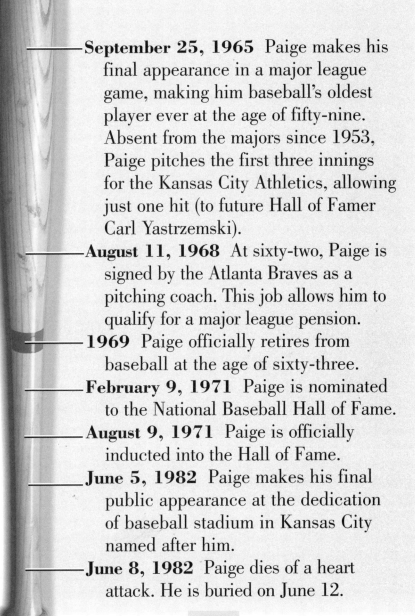

September 25, 1965 Paige makes his final appearance in a major league game, making him baseball's oldest player ever at the age of fifty-nine. Absent from the majors since 1953, Paige pitches the first three innings for the Kansas City Athletics, allowing just one hit (to future Hall of Famer Carl Yastrzemski).

August 11, 1968 At sixty-two, Paige is signed by the Atlanta Braves as a pitching coach. This job allows him to qualify for a major league pension.

1969 Paige officially retires from baseball at the age of sixty-three.

February 9, 1971 Paige is nominated to the National Baseball Hall of Fame.

August 9, 1971 Paige is officially inducted into the Hall of Fame.

June 5, 1982 Paige makes his final public appearance at the dedication of baseball stadium in Kansas City named after him.

June 8, 1982 Paige dies of a heart attack. He is buried on June 12.

Glossary

barnstorming The practice of touring throughout the country to play baseball games against other traveling teams rather than being associated with one city and a home field.

bee ball Also known as pea ball. One of Satchel Paige's fastballs, thrown so fast that it made a buzzing sound.

East-West All-Star Game An annual championship game played in the Negro leagues between teams of the eastern and western halves of the country.

ERA (earned run average) The average number of runs earned against a pitcher per inning.

exhibition game A game played off-season that does not count toward any championship but is designed to generate interest in and enthusiasm for the sport.

hesitation pitch One of Satchel Paige's trademark pitches, in which he put his foot down before he threw the ball, making it look like he had already thrown it and causing batters to swing too early.

integrate Open to all races, without restriction or discrimination.

Jim Crow laws Laws intended to keep the races separated from each other. These laws established separate institutions for whites and other races, and the white institutions were usually of higher quality.

major leagues One of two groups of teams (the National League and the American League) at the highest level of professional baseball.

minor leagues Groups of teams at a lower level of professional baseball. The minor leagues serve as a training ground for young players who often move up to the majors as their skills develop.

National Baseball Hall of Fame A not-for-profit educational institution dedicated to the history of baseball and honoring players who have made outstanding contributions to the game. Based in Cooperstown, New York.

Negro leagues Groups of African American baseball teams.

Negro National League A Negro baseball league, first established by Rube Foster in 1920.

rookie A player in his or her first year on a team.

scout A person who travels around the country looking for talented new players for sports teams.

semiprofessional Teams in which players have other jobs and only play baseball part-time.

shutout A game in which one side does not score.

windup The movements of a pitcher before he or she throws the ball.

World Series A series of games played each fall between the winning teams of the National League and the American League to decide the championship of the major leagues.

For More Information

Black Baseball.Com
P.O. Box 1122
Holly Springs, GA 30142-1122
Web site: http://www.blackbaseball.com
e-mail: info@blackbaseball.com

National Baseball Hall of Fame
   and Museum
25 Main Street
P.O. Box 590
Cooperstown, NY 13326
(888) HALL-OF-FAME (425-5633)
Web site: http://www.baseballhalloffame.org

Negro Leagues Baseball Museum
1616 E. 18th Street
Kansas City, MO 64108-1646
(816) 221-1920
Web site: http://www.nlbm.com

**Society for American Baseball Research
(SABR) Negro Leagues Committee
Newsletter**
Dick Clark, editor
1080 Hull St.
Ypsilanti, MI 48198-6472

Videos

Baseball—A Film by Ken Burns. Turner Home
Entertainment, 1994.

Web Sites

CBS Sportsline: Satchel Paige
http://cbs.sportsline.com/u/baseball/bol/
ballplayers/P/Paige_Satchel.html

A Look at the Negro Leagues: Satchel Paige

http://www.blackbaseball.com/players/paige.htm

Negro League Player Bios: Satchel Paige

http://www.execpc.com/~sshivers/paige.html

For Further Reading

Bruce, Janet. *The Kansas City Monarchs: Champions of Black Baseball*. Lawrence, KS: University Press of Kansas, 1985.

Chadwick, Bruce. *When the Game Was Black and White: The Illustrated History of Baseball's Negro Leagues*. New York: Abbeville Press, 1992.

Cline-Ransome, Lesa. *Satchel Paige*. New York: Simon and Schuster, 2000.

McKissack, Patricia C., and Frederick L. McKissack Jr. *Black Diamond: The Story of the Negro Baseball Leagues*. New York: Scholastic, 1998.

Paige, Leroy (Satchel), and David Lipman. *Maybe I'll Pitch Forever*. Lincoln, NE: University of Nebraska Press, 1993.

Peterson, Robert. *Only the Ball Was White: A History of Legendary Black Players and All-Black Professional Teams.* New York: Gramercy, 1999.

Ribowsky, Mark. *A Complete History of the Negro Leagues, 1884–1955.* Secaucus, NJ: The Citadel Press, 1997.

Ribowsky, Mark. *Don't Look Back: Satchel Paige in the Shadows of Baseball.* Cambridge, MA: Da Capo Press, 2000.

Ritter, Lawrence S. *Leagues Apart: The Men and Times of the Negro Baseball Leagues.* New York: Mulberry Books, 1999.

Shirley, David. *Satchel Paige.* New York: Chelsea House Publishers, 1993.

Sterry, David, and Arrielle Eckstut, eds. *Satchel Sez: The Wit, Wisdom, and World of Leroy "Satchel" Paige.* New York: Three Rivers Press, 2001.

Index

About the Author

Julie Schmidt was born in New Jersey and raised in New York state, Zambia, and Hong Kong. She currently resides in New York City, where she works as an editor and a freelance writer.

Photo Credits

Cover, pp. 18, 24, 43, 46, 55, 60, 72 © Corbis; pp. 4, 7, 33, 48, 69, 74, 79, 83, 87, 89, 92, 94 © AP/Wide World Photos; pp. 10, 14 © Library of Congress; pp. 23, 27, 29, 37, 39, 53, 65, 66 © New York Public Library; pp. 77, 91 © Hulton Archive.

Designer

Nelson Sá